Studying Snowflakes

Joseph Otterman

Smithsonian

Consultants

Brian Mandell
Program Specialist
Smithsonian Science Education Center

Amy Zoque
STEM Coordinator and Instructional Coach
Vineyard STEM School
Ontario Montclair School District

Publishing Credits

Rachelle Cracchiolo, M.S.Ed., *Publisher*
Conni Medina, M.A.Ed., *Editor in Chief*
Diana Kenney, M.A.Ed., NBCT, *Series Developer*
Emily R. Smith, M.A.Ed., *Content Director*
Véronique Bos, *Creative Director*
Robin Erickson, *Art Director*
Michelle Jovin, M.A., *Associate Editor*
Mindy Duits, *Senior Graphic Designer*
Smithsonian Science Education Center

Image Credits: p.11 Dorling Kindersley/Science Source; p.16 Philippe Psaila/Science Source; all other images from iStock and/or Shutterstock.

Library of Congress Cataloging-in-Publication Data

Names: Rice, Dona, author. | Smithsonian Institution.
Title: Studying snowflakes / Dona Herweck Rice.
Description: Huntington Beach, CA : Teacher Created Materials, 2019. |
  Audience: K to grade 3. | Copyrighted 2020 by the Smithsonian
Institution.
  | Identifiers: LCCN 2018049794 (print) | LCCN 2018057686 (ebook) | ISBN
  9781493868995 (eBook) | ISBN 9781493866595 (pbk.)
Subjects: LCSH: Snowflakes--Juvenile literature. | Snow--Juvenile literature.
Classification: LCC QC926.37 (ebook) | LCC QC926.37 .R53 2019 (print) |
DDC
  551.57/84--dc23
LC record available at https://lccn.loc.gov/2018049794

Teacher Created Materials

5301 Oceanus Drive
Huntington Beach, CA 92649-1030
www.tcmpub.com
ISBN 978-1-4938-6659-5

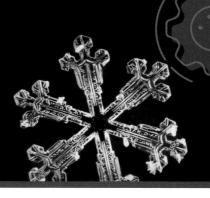

Table of Contents

3

From Dust to Snowflake

It starts with a speck of dust on a freezing day. A drop of cold water grabs onto the speck. The drop becomes an **ice crystal**. The ice crystal grows and grows.

Dust and water grow into an ice crystal.

ice crystals

The ice crystal becomes heavier than the air as it grows. It falls through the sky. It falls with other ice crystals. They are alike, but each one is different. They are unique. They are snowflakes!

Ice crystals are often called "snowflakes."

Snowflake Symmetry

Most snowflakes are **symmetrical**. This means if you fold the shape in half, both sides will match.

7

Precipitation

Snowflakes are one type of precipitation. There are also other types.

All precipitation starts as frozen water in the sky. Then, it falls to the earth. It can be liquid like rain. It can be solid like snow.

Types of Precipitation

Snow stays frozen.	Sleet melts. It freezes again in the air.	Freezing rain melts. It freezes again on the ground.	Rain melts.

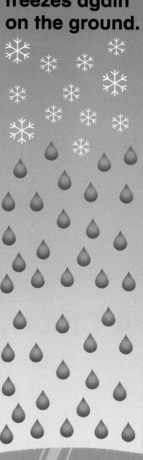

Precipitation forms in clouds. Clouds are made of water. The water in clouds forms crystals in the freezing air.

The crystals may grow. They may grab onto other crystals. They turn into ice or snow. Then, they fall to the ground.

Science & Technology

A Cloudy Idea

Clouds are mostly made up of tiny water drops. **Gravity** can make the drops fall to the earth. That is rain. Snow or hail form when the water drops freeze.

Water drops can freeze into snowflakes that fall to the earth.

Shape Up

Snowflakes catch on our hair and mittens. They stick to our clothes. That is partly because of their shapes. Ice crystals are covered with spiky parts. They are all formed the same way. But they have different shapes.

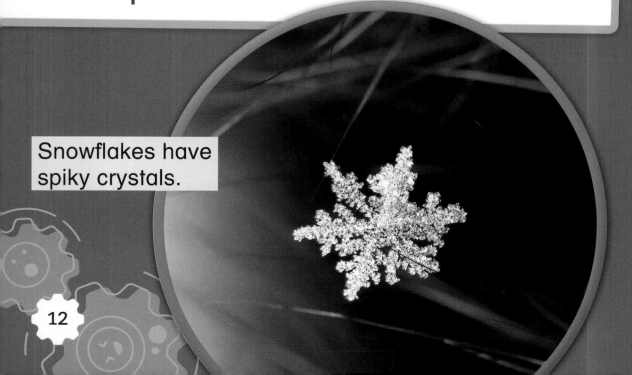

Snowflakes have spiky crystals.

The shapes of snowflakes cause them to stick to this mitten.

Long ago, **scientists** made a chart. It showed snowflake shapes. It had seven groups of shapes.

These scientists found that weather causes the shapes. The **temperature** of the air will change the shape. The amount of water in the air will change it too.

This thermometer shows that the temperature of the air is cold enough for snow.

Snowflake Shapes

One snowflake shape is called *stellar dendrite*. *Stellar* means "star." *Dendrite* means "tree." The shape looks like a star made of trees.

Over time, scientists found more snowflake shapes. Now, they sort ice crystal shapes into 39 main groups! But there are lots of shapes in each group. In fact, there are more shapes than you can think of!

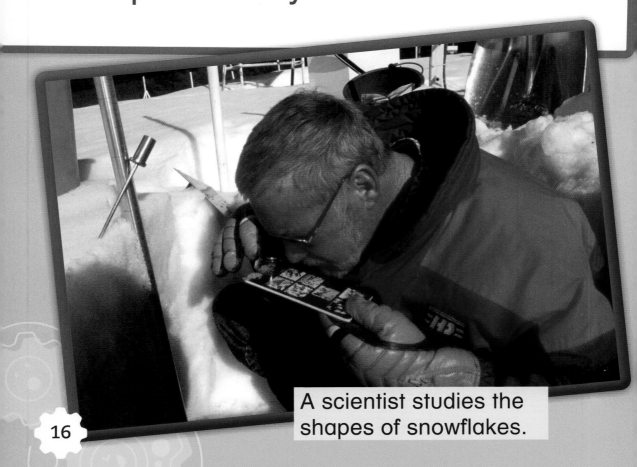

A scientist studies the shapes of snowflakes.

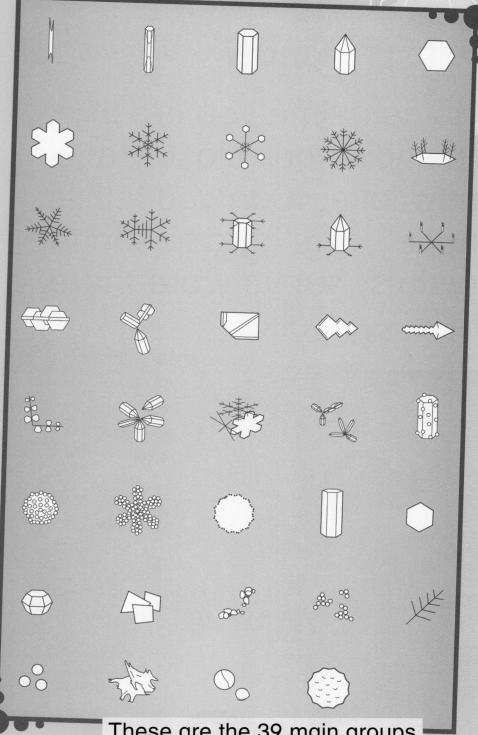

These are the 39 main groups
of ice crystal shapes.

17

Let It Snow

The next time you are in the snow, look closely at a snowflake. Can you tell its shape? It is hard to see the crystals, but they are there. Hello, crystals!

STEAM CHALLENGE

The Problem

You are going to the Arctic to study snowflakes. First, you must build an igloo to live in. It will be made of blocks of snow. What shape should your igloo be so that it stays strong?

The Goals

- Make a model of your igloo with marshmallows, sugar cubes, tape, and/or glue.
- Make the igloo hollow so there is room for you to live inside.
- Make the igloo strong enough to hold a metal washer without breaking.

1 Research and Brainstorm

Why do snowflakes stick together? Why can igloos only be made in freezing places?

2 Design and Build

Draw your plan. How will it work? What materials will you use? Build your model!

3 Test and Improve

Place a metal washer on top of your igloo for one minute. Did the igloo stay whole? Did it break? Can you make it better? Try again.

4 Reflect and Share

How big do you think an igloo can be and still stand? What else could be built from snow or ice?

Glossary

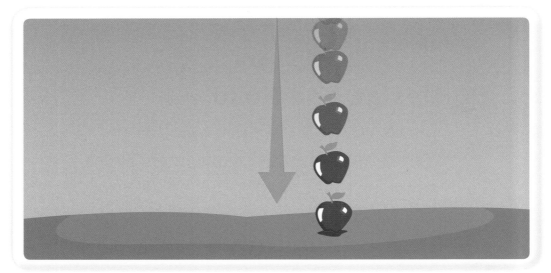

gravity

ice crystal

scientists

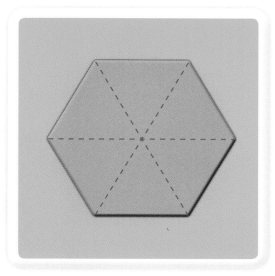

symmetrical

temperature

Career Advice
from Smithsonian

Do you want to study types of weather?
Here are some tips to get you started.

"Take notes of different types of weather you see. Look for patterns and spend time outdoors!" — *Dr. Don E. Wilson, Curator Emeritus*

"Weather affects so many parts of our lives. Study science and read weather reports. See if you can predict what types of weather will happen next." — *Brian Mandell, Program Specialist*